Contents

Some words are printed in bold, **like this**. You can find out what they mean in the glossary.

A strange sort of race

It is a very strange sort of car race. All the cars are tiny. Some look like smooth, silver tubes, others are bubble-shaped. Some look like they were built using pieces from a scrap heap. Some of the cars sound like sewing machines or lawnmowers, while others make hardly any noise at all. The strangest thing of all is that the winning car is the last to finish. What sort of race is this? It is the 2005 European Shell Eco Marathon. Every year there are Eco Marathons in Europe and the United States. Groups of students from colleges and schools race cars that are very fuel-efficient, to see which one uses the least fuel.

The winner of the 2005 race was *PAC-Car II*, built by students from Switzerland. Later that year it set a world record by travelling 5,385 km (3,346 miles) on one litre (1.76 pints) of fuel. This is about 300 times better than the most fuel-efficient road car.

Swiss students test out the *PAC-Car II*, the world's most fuel-efficient car.

Creating PAC-Car II

PAC-Car II was based on an earlier car, PAC-Car I, which was the first Eco Marathon car to be powered by a hydrogen **fuel cell** (see page 42). For PAC-Car II, the students greatly reduced the car's overall size and weight. They used computer modelling to design an extremely **aerodynamic** body shape. They ran many practical tests to see just how small and low they could make the car, while still allowing the driver to see and move. The two wheels at the front of the car are fixed, while the single rear wheel steers. The students experimented with the exact angle of the front wheels to produce the least **friction** with the road.

Using less energy

There are two important reasons why we need vehicles that use less fuel – and why we need to use less energy altogether. Firstly, if we do not use fuel more carefully, we will run out. Secondly, our overuse of fuel is contributing to global **climate change**.

The main fuels we use for transport, heating, and to make electricity are oil, coal, and gas – the **fossil fuels**. Every year, the amount of fuel we use rises. The world's population is increasing and we are producing more and more machines that need energy to work. However, the amount of fossil fuels in the world is limited. Experts think we are reaching peak production levels for oil and that in less than 40 years, oil could run out altogether. Gas and coal will last longer, but eventually they will also run out. We need to cut down on energy use to make fossil fuel supplies last longer. At the same time, we need to find other sources of energy that will not run out.

Pollution and climate change

There is a more urgent reason for reducing our use of fossil fuels. When fossil fuels burn, they release polluting gases into the atmosphere. The worst of these are sulphur and nitrogen oxides. These gases can cause breathing problems. They can also cause **acid rain**, which damages plants and wildlife in rivers and lakes. The gases can cause smog (pollution fog), and in sunlight they react with other substances to produce toxic (poisonous) chemicals.

Carbon dioxide (CO_2) is another gas produced when fossil fuels burn. As a result, levels of carbon dioxide in the atmosphere are increasing. This build-up is causing changes to the world's climate. Overall, the world is getting warmer, but the effects are not the same everywhere. In some places, the climate is getting wetter and there is more flooding. Other places are having much less rainfall, which is causing **droughts**. Everywhere there are more extremes in the weather.

THE SCIENCE YOU LEARN: WHERE DO FOSSIL FUELS COME FROM?

Fossil fuels are the remains of plants and animals that lived millions of years ago. Nearly all coal was formed around 300 million years ago when parts of the Earth were covered by huge, swampy forests. When the forest trees died, they sank in to the swamp, and became covered by layers of mud and rock. Over many years, a combination of heat and pressure turned the plants into coal. Oil and gas formed in a similar way, but from the remains of small animals and plants buried on the bottom of shallow lakes and seas.

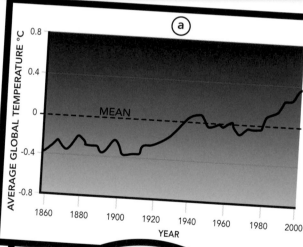

These graphs show a) the average global temperature and b) carbon dioxide levels in the air over the past 150 years. Both carbon dioxide levels and average temperature have risen over this time period.

Waste and water

Another major pollution problem is the enormous amount of waste we produce each year. In most countries this waste goes in landfill sites (it is buried in the ground). However, the amount of space available for landfill is limited, and landfill sites can produce polluting gases and chemicals that leak into water supplies. We need to find new ways to deal with waste and in particular reduce our waste.

As the climate gets warmer, it becomes more important to save water. Currently in the UK, people use an average of 150 litres (33 gallons) of water per day. In the United States, the figure is around 575 litres (126 gallons) per day. We need to reduce the amount of water we use, or we will use up the water supplies in rivers, lakes, and in the ground.

Khlongs (canals) run through the heart of the city of Bangkok, Thailand. The water in them is heavily polluted with all kinds of waste. But some people still use the *khlongs* for bathing and washing.

Designing greener cars and buildings

If we carry on using fossil fuels and water the way we are now, the problems of pollution and water shortages will quickly get worse.

In this book we will look at how we can design buildings and vehicles that are greener – use less energy and water, and produce less waste and carbon dioxide. We will see how scientists, engineers, and others are tackling the challenges of climate change and pollution.

Green buildings

Buildings use an enormous amount of energy. They use energy for heating in cold weather and cooling in hot weather. Lights use energy, as does the hot water system and all the devices that run on electricity, from electric cookers to fax machines. Factories need energy for heavy machinery, furnaces, and other equipment. We could save a huge amount of energy if we redesigned buildings to be more energy-efficient.

Insulation

The main use of energy in most buildings is for heating. Often, much of the heat leaks out through areas with poor **insulation**. Designers and builders can reduce energy use by improving a building's insulation. The walls and roof of a building can be insulated fairly easily. It is less easy to insulate windows, and they are often the main route for heat to escape from a building. However, great improvements have been made in window insulation. Modern, low-energy windows are **triple-glazed**, and gas fills the gaps between the panes. The glass can also be given a coating that allows light to pass through but reflects heat back into the building.

THE SCIENCE YOU LEARN: CARBON FOOTPRINT

The term "**carbon footprint**" is often used in news stories about green issues. Whenever we use fossil fuels, carbon dioxide is produced. Therefore, the amount of energy we use can be expressed as an amount of carbon dioxide produced. This is our carbon footprint. The average carbon footprint of a person in the UK is 12 tonnes (13 tons) of carbon dioxide per year, while the average for a U.S. citizen is 19 tonnes (21 tons) per year. Australians have an average carbon footprint of 22 tonnes (24 tons) per year, while in countries such as Brazil and Indonesia the footprint is much lower at only about 2 tonnes (2.2 tons) per year.

A house or other building can also have a carbon footprint, although an efficient, energy-saving building can be **carbon-neutral**. This means that the building's net emissions are zero.

This thermogram of a row of houses shows hotter areas as orange or red and cooler areas as blue. It shows that the house in the middle of the row has effective roof insulation, and is losing far less heat energy through the roof.

Free heat

If it is well designed, a building can harness and use free heat from the Sun. Warming a building in this way is known as passive solar design. This type of design makes use of conduction, convection, and **radiation** (see box).

Passive solar design works best for small buildings for which heating is the main energy expense. Architects design long, rectangular buildings, with the long sides facing north and south. In winter, large areas of windows on the south side of the building gain heat energy from the Sun. This warms the air in the house. The north-facing side of the house should have no windows at all. For this arrangement to work, there must be efficient air circulation inside the house, so that the heat does not all stay on the south-facing side. There must also be a way for daylight to get into north-facing rooms.

A passive solar building design also needs to include materials with high thermal mass. Thermal mass is the ability of a material to absorb heat energy. Materials with a high thermal mass, such as concrete slabs, brick walls, and tile floors, soak up sunlight by day and then radiate it out as heat at night. The materials have a high **heat capacity**.

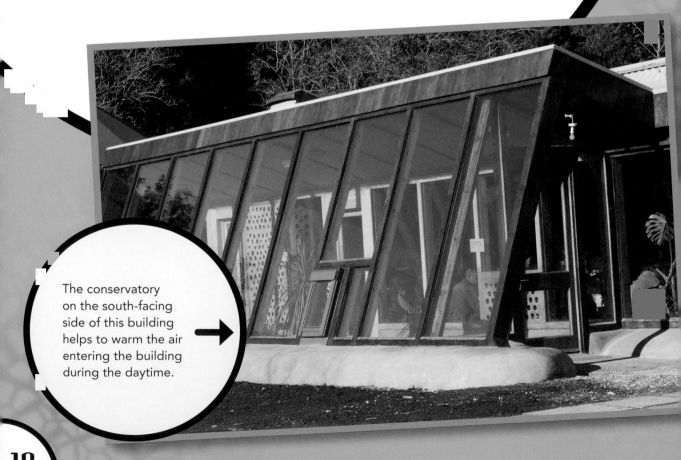

The conservatory on the south-facing side of this building helps to warm the air entering the building during the daytime.

To prevent overheating in summer, the roof should overhang the south-facing windows. In summer, the Sun is higher in the sky, and the overhang cuts out direct sunlight. A screen of deciduous trees (trees that shed their leaves in winter) can also provide shade in summer, while allowing sunlight through in winter.

Another easy way to improve solar heating is to build a conservatory on the south-facing side. During the day, the conservatory is warm, and doors connecting the building to the conservatory are kept open. At night, the conservatory cools down, so doors into the building are shut.

THE SCIENCE YOU LEARN:
CONDUCTION, CONVECTION, AND RADIATION

Heat can move from place to place in three different ways, by conduction, convection, and radiation. A wood-burning stove heats a room using all three methods. The fire inside the stove heats the outer metal casing by conduction. Conduction is the way that heat travels through solid materials. Metals are good conductors of heat — they heat up (or cool down) quickly.

The outside of the stove radiates heat. Radiated heat is heat that travels in rays or waves, in a similar way to light. Heat from the Sun reaches us by radiation.

The warmed air around the stove expands and rises, and cooler air moves in to take its place. This begins a circular movement of air called a convection current. Convection currents spread heat through a liquid or a gas.

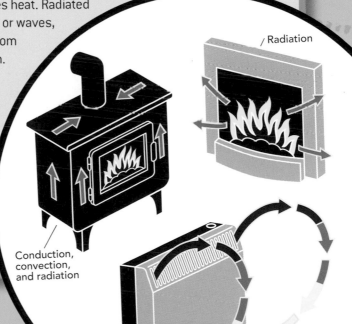

Radiation

Conduction, convection, and radiation

Convection

Keeping cool

In hot climates, cooling a building is the main energy cost. Usually, buildings are cooled with an air-conditioning system, but it is possible to design a building that cools itself.

The best shape for a self-cooling building is a long rectangle, with the long sides facing north and south. The main windows should be on the north side. The building needs a heavily insulated roof to keep out the direct heat of the Sun. Ventilation openings on the east and west sides allow a cooling breeze to pass through the building.

Portcullis House

Portcullis House in London (right) stays cool in hot weather without using air conditioning. The huge chimneys on its roof are part of an unpowered air-conditioning system that draws air through the building using natural convection flow. The design is based on a system that was used in the Eastgate building in Harare, Zimbabwe, built in 1996. The Eastgate's air conditioning system was modelled on the way that termites build their self-cooling mounds!

The ground is usually cooler than the air above it. Therefore, for further cooling, an underground pipe or chamber can be built. Air cools as it passes through the pipe and enters the building. Warm air inside the building rises and leaves the building through vents and chimneys in the roof. As the warm air leaves, it draws in more cool air from underground.

In large office buildings, even those in cooler climates, the heat generated by people and machinery keeps the air warm. Cooling systems are usually needed rather than heating systems. Architects can use passive cooling systems like the one described above to help cool a large building. Often, electric fans are needed to make sure that cool air reaches all parts of the building. This still uses far less energy than air conditioning.

One simple way to save water at home is to collect rainwater in a water butt. This water can then be used in the garden.

Saving water

Buildings can be designed to save water as well as energy. Many new designs of toilets, showers, and taps use less water than older designs. For example, taps that produce a spray use less water than those that produce a solid stream. Washing machines that use less water also use less energy. This is because it takes a lot of energy to heat water.

Another way to save water is to collect rainwater and use it in the garden. Some green buildings have water purification systems. Water from sinks and baths is fed into a reed bed that cleans it to be used again. Some homes have systems to collect rainwater for flushing toilets.

Many energy-saving buildings use materials that soak up heat. The ability of a material to absorb heat is called its heat capacity. Materials like stone and concrete have a high heat capacity, while the heat capacity of metals is low. Water has a very high heat capacity, as this experiment shows.

SAFETY WARNING: This experiment involves fire. Do not try it without an adult present.

Equipment
- two balloons
- one candle
- matches or a lighter
- water

Procedure

1. Blow up one of the balloons and tie it off. Light the candle. What do you think will happen if you put the balloon in the candle flame? Carefully, just touch the balloon to the tip of the candle flame. What happens?

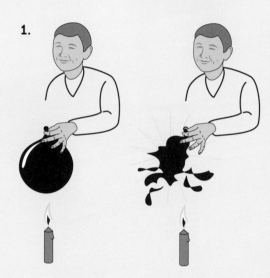

2. Fill the second balloon with water and tie it off. As before, carefully touch the balloon to the tip of the candle flame. What happens this time?

Results

When the balloon is full of air, it bursts as soon as you put it in the candle flame. However, you can hold the water-filled balloon in the candle flame for 30 seconds or more, and it does not pop. This is because of water's high heat capacity. The water absorbs the heat from the candle, so the surface of the balloon doesn't become hot enough to pop.

Heat capacity

Understanding heat capacity is important for engineers and many designers. A saucepan, for example, should have a thick base with a high heat capacity. In this design, the base quickly absorbs the heat of the burners and releases it more gradually into the food.

Water's ability to absorb heat is used in the cooling system of a car engine. The engine produces heat every time fuel is burned in one of the cylinders. To stop the car overheating and keep it at the best working temperature, the engine is cooled by water circulating around the cylinders, pistons, and other parts of the engine.

CUTTING EDGE: SMART BUILDINGS

Large buildings often have complex systems to control when the heating and air-conditioning systems turn on and off. In a smart building, the control system does much more than this. It might **monitor** the temperature inside and outside the building, closing off ventilation when it is cold and opening it when it is hot. It may also monitor light levels, and turn electric lights on and off depending on how much natural light is available.

In a hotel or office, a smart control system might even use room booking information to automatically turn on lights and heating or cooling systems just before a room is due to be used. It would then turn them off when the room is empty. A good smart control system can reduce energy bills for a building by up to 60 percent.

Alternative energy

Even the most energy-efficient building uses some energy. Energy is needed to heat water and to power lights and other electric devices. For most buildings, this energy comes from fossil fuels. However, it is possible for a building to produce its own energy, without using fossil fuels.

THE SCIENCE YOU LEARN: ENERGY BASICS

One important law of physics states that we cannot make energy or destroy it. Whenever we use energy, we either transfer it from one place to another, or change it from one kind of energy into another. Fuels, such as oil or natural gas, are stores of energy. The energy is locked up in the chemical bonds of the oil or gas molecules. When a fuel is burned, some of the chemical bonds are broken, and this releases heat energy. The heat can be used to warm a room for example, or to heat water for a bath or shower. The chemical energy in the fuel has been changed into heat energy.

This diagram shows the release of energy when chemical bonds are broken during combustion.

FUEL

OXYGEN

EXHAUST

HEAT

HEAT

Heat from light

One readily available energy source is sunlight. In warm countries especially, sunlight can supply a building with both electricity and heating.

Solar heating panels are designed to capture sunlight and use its energy to heat water. A simple panel consists of a flat black metal plate covered by a pane of glass. The sunlight passes through the glass and is absorbed by the black metal plate. Dark colours are very good at absorbing heat radiation. The sunlight heats the black metal plate and the glass stops the heat escaping back into the air. Instead, the heat warms pipes underneath the metal plate. The pipes carry water or another liquid. The warm liquid heated in the solar panel can then be used to warm water in a hot-water tank, or to heat radiators.

Simple solar heating panels work well in warm countries. However, in cooler areas this type of panel does not provide enough heat to be useful. A better kind of solar heating panel is an array (collection) of black vacuum tubes. The best **vacuum** tube solar panels are very efficient. They can convert around 93 percent of sunlight into heat energy. These types of solar heating panels are even used in science bases at the Antarctic, where the temperature can fall as low as −40°C.

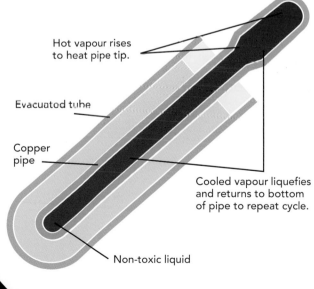

Hot vapour rises
to heat pipe tip.

Evacuated tube

Copper
pipe

Cooled vapour liquefies
and returns to bottom
of pipe to repeat cycle.

Non-toxic liquid

Vacuum tube solar panes (right) are double-walled glass tubes with a vacuum between the two layers of glass. In the centre of each tube is a liquid. The Sun's energy heats the liquid in the centre of the vacuum tube. The vacuum tubes do not let heat out. The heated liquid warms water for the building.

Solar power

Another type of solar panel is the **photovoltaic** (PV) solar panel. PV panels convert sunlight into electricity. They are made from **semiconductor** materials such as silicon. When light falls on the materials, they produce an electric current. An array of PV panels on a building's roof can provide more than half the total amount of electricity used in the building.

The heat produced by solar heating panels can be stored efficiently in a well-insulated hot water tank. Any extra electricity produced by PV panels can charge up batteries. However, many buildings with PV panels are connected to the mains electricity grid. When the panels produce more electricity than is being used in the building, the spare electricity flows into the mains electricity grid and can be used elsewhere.

Ordinary PV panels convert around 15 percent of the light that falls on them into electricity. The panels are also expensive to make. It can take more than 10 years for PV panels to save enough electricity to earn back their initial cost. However, PV panels do not produce pollution or carbon dioxide, and sunlight will not run out for around five billion years.

An engineer fits PV panels to a house roof. The panels must be fitted to a specially made framework.

Solar cells

In 1839, French scientist Alexandre-Edmond Becquerel (1820–1891) discovered that some metals produce an electric voltage when light falls on them. This is the photovoltaic effect. Until the 1950s, **selenium** was used in solar cells, but these cells were so inefficient that their only real use was in camera light meters.

In the early 1950s, U.S. scientist Daryl Chapin (1906–1995) began trying to improve solar cells at Bell Laboratories in the United States. His research using selenium got nowhere, but then an accidental discovery helped him along. Two scientists at the laboratory, Calvin Fuller (1902–1994) and Gerald Pearson (1905–1986), were developing new electronic devices using silicon. In one experiment, they produced a silicon-based device that produced an electric current when it was lit up.

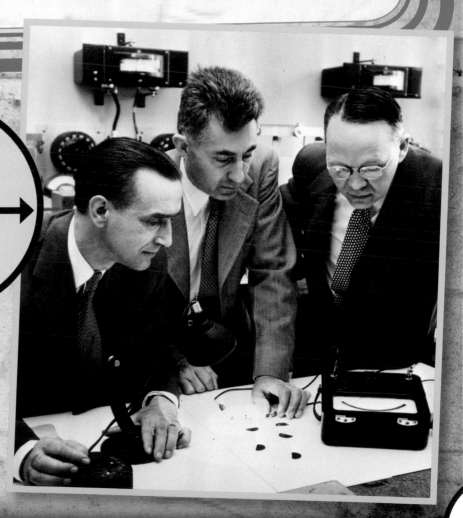

Gerald Pearson (left), Daryl Chapin (centre), and Calvin Fuller are seen here working on the development of the first practical solar cell.

Pumping heat

A heat pump is an efficient way to heat a building. Heat naturally flows from warmer objects to colder ones. When we take a pizza out of the oven it is piping hot, but an hour later it will be around the same temperature as the rest of the room. However, by putting in a small amount of energy, it is possible to pump heat from a colder area to a warmer one. A fridge is a type of heat pump. It cools down the air inside the fridge. To do this it uses a working fluid that soaks up heat inside the fridge, then dumps it outside. A heat pump for a building works in reverse. It soaks up heat from the outside environment, then dumps this heat inside the building.

For a heat pump to work, it needs a heat sink. A heat sink is something with a very high heat capacity that contains a large amount of heat energy. Luckily, every building has access to at least one very good heat sink – the ground. Water (a pond or a stream) also makes a good heat sink. Although the heat sink is at a low temperature (lower than the inside of the building), it still contains huge amounts of heat energy. The heat pump soaks up some of this energy and carries it into the building.

Like a fridge, a heat pump uses a working fluid to operate. The working fluid starts out as a liquid flowing through a narrow tube at high pressure. The fluid flows into a bigger tube. Under lower pressure, the liquid cools down to become cooler than the heat sink. It is therefore warmed as it passes through the heat sink. The liquid warms up and **evaporates** (turns into a gas).

THE SCIENCE YOU LEARN:
FROM GAS TO LIQUID AND BACK AGAIN

When a liquid evaporates, heat energy is needed to break the connections between the liquid particles. Therefore, when a liquid evaporates, it cools – the liquid takes heat from the environment. This is why sweating cools us down. When a gas condenses, it releases energy. Therefore, if a gas condenses, it becomes hotter.

As the pipe goes back into the building, it narrows again. The pump compresses the gas as it flows into this narrow pipe, and this makes the gas **condense** (turn into a liquid). When a gas condenses, it warms up. So when the working fluid flows into the building, it is hotter than the building itself. This heat can be used to warm the air, or to heat water in a hot-water tank.

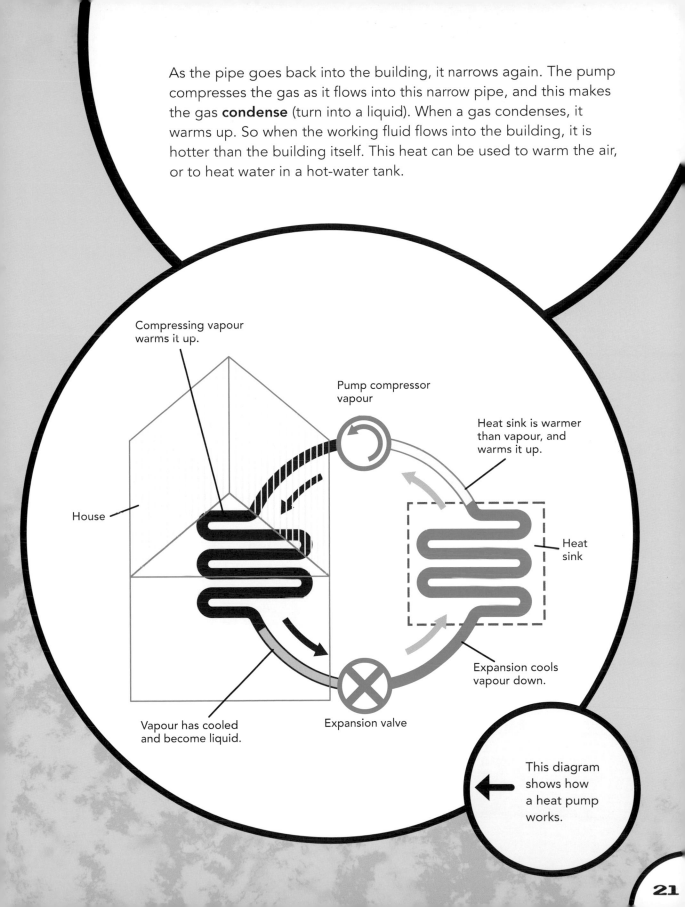

Compressing vapour warms it up.

Pump compressor vapour

Heat sink is warmer than vapour, and warms it up.

House

Heat sink

Vapour has cooled and become liquid.

Expansion valve

Expansion cools vapour down.

This diagram shows how a heat pump works.

Energy from nowhere?

In a heat pump system, the pump that moves the working fluid through the pipes needs energy to work. However, the energy that it uses is less than the heat energy it pumps into the building. Overall, a heat pump seems to be making energy – how can this be possible? In fact, energy is not being made. The heat sink loses as much heat as the building gains. If the heat sink was something small, for example a bowl of water, it would quickly cool as it lost heat until it reached the same temperature as the working fluid. At this point the heat pump would stop working. However, the heat sink is huge – effectively it could be the whole of the Earth if using the ground. The cooling effect of the working fluid therefore has almost no effect on the temperature of the heat sink.

A heat pump is most effective in a low-energy building. Good insulation in this type of building means that the heat pumped in is not lost through windows and as leaking air. It therefore only needs a small amount of heat energy to keep it warm.

THE SCIENCE YOU LEARN:
KINETIC AND POTENTIAL ENERGY

Kinetic energy and **potential energy** are the two basic energy types. Kinetic energy is the energy of movement. The faster something moves, the more kinetic energy it has. Heat is a form of kinetic energy. It is the energy of the particles (the **atoms** and molecules) that make up any substance. If something is hot, the particles in it are moving faster than if it is cold.

Potential energy is stored energy. A ball at the top of a hill has potential energy, because if you let it go, it will roll down the hill. This is gravitational potential energy. A spring or an elastic band has stored energy when it is stretched – this is elastic potential energy. A fuel has chemical potential energy because there is energy stored in the chemical bonds within the fuel particles.

This skateboarder has potential energy, which he is about to convert into kinetic energy. As he launches himself down the ramp, the force of gravity pulls him downwards at increasing speed.

Green materials

Reducing the amount of energy that a building uses solves only half the problem. Energy is also required to make the building materials. This energy is known as the embodied energy of a building. By choosing the right materials, it is possible to reduce even this kind of energy.

Embodied energy

The embodied energy of a typical building can be between 10 and 30 times the amount of energy used in the building in a year.

Let us look at the production of a steel girder for the framework of a large office building. Steel is made from iron. Iron comes from iron **ore**. Firstly, the iron ore has to be mined, then transported to a blast furnace where it is heated to extract the iron. Next, the iron is transported to a steel works where it is heated with oxygen in another furnace to produce steel. The steel is formed into a girder and transported to the construction site. Finally, the girder must be lifted and fixed into place. All these processes involve energy. The exact amount of energy involved varies depending on how far the iron ore travels from the mine to the construction site. If a material is transported a long way, it can double its embodied energy.

Many modern building materials, such as concrete, steel, plastic, and aluminium, have a high embodied energy. Aluminium has the highest embodied energy of all because purifying the metal from its ore uses huge amounts of electricity.

Steel is one of the most widespread building materials. Unfortunately, it has a high-embodied energy: it takes a lot of energy to make the steel, shape it, and transport it to the building site.

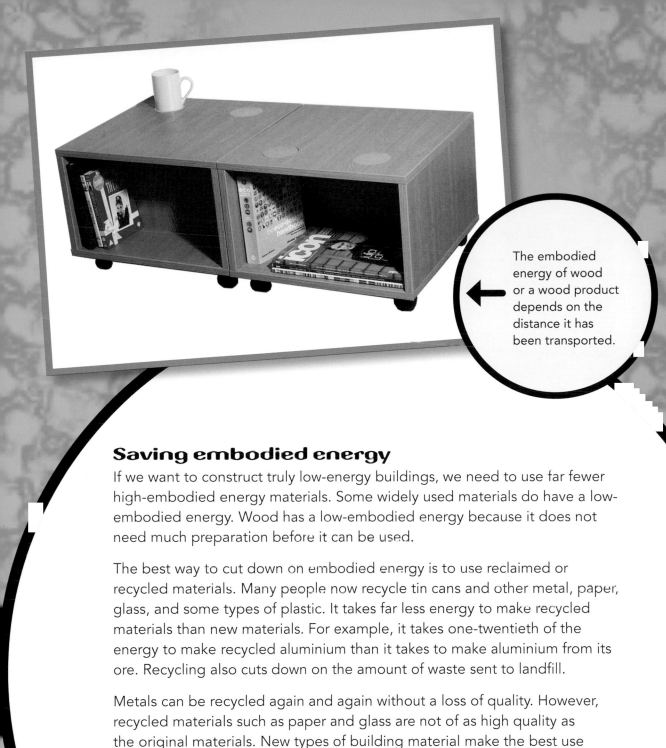

The embodied energy of wood or a wood product depends on the distance it has been transported.

Saving embodied energy

If we want to construct truly low-energy buildings, we need to use far fewer high-embodied energy materials. Some widely used materials do have a low-embodied energy. Wood has a low-embodied energy because it does not need much preparation before it can be used.

The best way to cut down on embodied energy is to use reclaimed or recycled materials. Many people now recycle tin cans and other metal, paper, glass, and some types of plastic. It takes far less energy to make recycled materials than new materials. For example, it takes one-twentieth of the energy to make recycled aluminium than it takes to make aluminium from its ore. Recycling also cuts down on the amount of waste sent to landfill.

Metals can be recycled again and again without a loss of quality. However, recycled materials such as paper and glass are not of as high quality as the original materials. New types of building material make the best use of recycled materials. Warmcel, for example, is a very good, cheap type of insulation made from old newspaper. There are also new types of particle board made from recycled plastics, which are proving to be very useful building materials.

Local materials

Cutting down on transport costs can greatly reduce embodied energy. For example, making concrete on-site uses half the energy of using pre-cast concrete.

In some low-energy buildings, architects have experimented with less common materials with low-embodied energy. Rammed-earth construction, for example, is a way of building walls using earth mixed with a small amount of cement to bind it together. Walls made this way are strong and long-lasting in dry climates.

The walls of this house were built using rammed-earth construction. This is an excellent low-energy material for dry climates.

CASE STUDY

Reusing tyres

Every year, millions and millions of used car tyres are dumped. It is very difficult to find a use for tyre rubber. It cannot be melted down, and it is hard to chemically combine rubber with other materials.

Many uses for recycled tyres are being developed. In Australia, a research company called Molectra has developed a process for producing many different products from recycled tyres. Most commonly, the rubber is ground up into either a powder or crumbs. Crumb rubber can be used to create a tough and slightly bouncy surface for use in children's playgrounds and sports tracks. It can also be used in road construction and as a sound insulator. Other products from tyres include re-bonded rubber, silicone tiles, oil, steel, jet fuel, and even a product to improve garden soil.

Bringing everything together

When architects design low-energy buildings, they combine **passive heating** and cooling, **green energy**, and low-embodied energy materials in their overall plan. By combining all these factors it is possible to construct buildings that have a carbon footprint of zero. Zero-energy buildings produce enough energy to offset the energy used for heating, lighting, and so on. If all our buildings were designed this way, it would go a long way towards solving our energy problems.

CASE STUDY

Bedzed

The Beddington Zero-Energy Development (Bedzed) is a carbon-neutral block of flats in London. The design includes super insulation and a passive heating and ventilation system that greatly reduces the energy needed to keep the building at a comfortable temperature. Solar cells provide some electricity, while a small, local, combined heat and power (CHP) station supplies both electricity and water heating. Many of the materials used in the building are recycled or reclaimed. Most of the steel was reclaimed from builders' yards within 56 km (35 miles) of the Bedzed site. Window frames are wooden rather than aluminium or plastic, because wood has a lower embodied energy, and wooden-framed windows proved to give the best insulation for the price.

The spinning chimneys on the roof of the Bedzed development are part of the ventilation system. The glass areas on the top storey provide passive heat from sunlight.

Greener transport

Transport is at the heart of modern life. Air transport allows people to fly anywhere in the world in a matter of hours. Sea transport carries goods across the oceans. Freight trains and trucks carry goods overland, while buses and passenger trains carry people. Cars give us our own personal form of transport, and the flexibility to travel where and when we choose.

However, the freedom and convenience of modern transport comes at a price. Petrol, diesel, and aircraft fuel are all made from oil. Together, these transport fuels produce almost one-third of our total carbon dioxide emissions. We need to find ways to reduce the amount of energy that vehicles use, and the amount of pollution they cause.

Shape and weight

Eco Marathon cars (see pages 4–5) save a lot of fuel by cutting down their weight and reducing **drag**. However, it is difficult to make weight savings in private cars, because large, powerful cars are a **status symbol**. The look of a car is also important to people, and streamlining sometimes takes second place to fashion, or the need to provide luggage space. However, the use of new technology has made it possible to improve streamlining. Computer-aided design (CAD) programs make it easier and quicker to experiment with new designs, and computer modelling can be used to test the streamlining properties of a design. Once a design has been tested on the computer, a prototype can be made using a process known as rapid prototyping. This involves using a machine that makes a scale model of the design directly from the CAD plans, building up the shape one thin layer at a time. The prototype can then be tested more conventionally, in a wind tunnel.

A new generation of aircraft designs called blended wing-body designs have been created in this way. In this design, the body has an aerofoil shape and produces its own **lift**. The aircraft has a reduced drag because the wings and body blend together in a smooth shape.

New concepts in ship design also reduce drag on the hull. Experiments have shown that with a particular shape of hull, air pumped over the surface can reduce drag by up to 40 percent. Russian shipbuilders have built several ships that use this system. Other researchers in Japan and the United States are experimenting with using air bubbles to reduce drag.

The Boeing X-48B is an experimental blended wing-body aircraft. The test aircraft first flew in July 2007.

Heat engines

Streamlining vehicles and cutting down their weight can make some energy savings. However, far larger energy savings can be made by improving vehicle engines. More than 60 percent of a car's waste energy is lost from the engine.

Petrol engines, diesel engines, and jet engines are all **internal combustion (IC) engines**. An internal combustion engine is a type of heat engine. Heat engines burn fuel to make heat, and the heat is used to move the vehicle along.

New, clean kinds of energy are being developed that will power vehicles without producing carbon dioxide (see pages 38–45). However, in the short term we need to improve IC engines. To work out how this can be done, we first need to understand how IC engines work.

How a petrol engine works

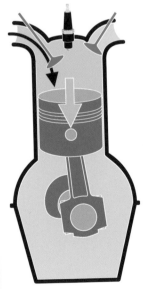  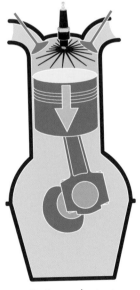 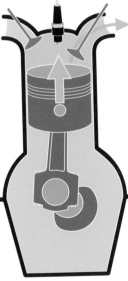

1. At the start of the process, fuel and air are drawn into the cylinder.

2. The piston moves up and compresses the mixture of fuel and air.

3. A spark starts the fuel burning. The gases expand and push the piston down.

4. As the piston rises again, waste gases are pushed out of the cylinder.

In an IC engine, fuel and air burn together in a closed space called a combustion chamber. When the fuel and air burn, they produce heat, and this makes the gases in the combustion chamber expand. The expanding gases do work – they push down a piston, and this turns a shaft called the crankshaft. The crankshaft turns the wheels of the car or train, or the propeller of a boat or ship. In a jet engine, the expanding gases are forced out of the engine through a nozzle in a high-speed jet. This jet of hot gases pushes the aircraft forwards.

THE SCIENCE YOU LEARN: EXPANDING AND CONTRACTING

What happens to a gas when it is heated? The scientist who first studied this was French physicist and balloonist, Jacques Charles (1746–1823), in 1787. The result of his experiments was a law, now known as Charles' Law. It states that as the temperature of a gas rises, its volume increases. Conversely, as the temperature of a gas drops, its volume decreases. This law can also be written as a mathematical formula.

↑
Jacques Charles made the first manned hydrogen balloon flight in Paris on 1 December 1783.

Cool as well as hot

If we look at the different types of IC engine, and other heat engines such as steam engines, we can see that they all have the same basic parts. There is the fuel, which heats up a working fluid (a gas or liquid), which expands to do work (usually moves something). However, this description leaves out an important point. When Sadi Carnot (1796–1832, see page 35) and other scientists studied heat engines, they realized that no heat engine can work without a cold sink. This does not mean that every engine needs a sink of cold water! It is simply a way to make sure the engine has a supply of cool working fluid that can be heated up by the fuel.

To see why we need a cold sink, let us look at how a steam turbine works. Steam turbines are used in many types of power station. They turn the electric generators. A boiler uses oil, gas, coal, or some other fuel to heat water and turn it into steam. High-pressure jets of steam are shot through the steam turbine, and turn the fan-like blades.

Cooling towers

All this is similar to any other heat engine. A fluid is heated, expands, and does work. In a power station, there is another step in the process. The steam is not just released into the air. It travels through pipes to a cooling tower, where it is cooled down to form liquid water. The water can then go back to the boiler and be heated again into steam.

Therefore, in a steam turbine, the cooling towers are the cold sink. In other engines, the cold sink is usually the outside world. A car engine constantly draws in cool air from outside, and pushes out hot air through the exhaust. A jet engine draws in cool air through fans at the front, and pushes out hot gases through the nozzle at the back. In both cases, the cold sink is the Earth's atmosphere.

The large, fat chimneys at this power station are cooling towers. They act as a "cold sink" by cooling the steam from the turbines.

Improving engines

The amount of energy we can get from an engine is limited by the difference between the temperature of the cold sink and the temperature of the gases once they have been heated. For most engines, the cold sink is the outside world, so we can't make it colder. Therefore, to make an engine more efficient, we need to make the combustion hotter. The best way to do this is to squash the mixture of fuel and air, because this heats it up.

A petrol engine uses a spark to set off combustion, and there is a limit to how much the mixture of fuel and air can be heated. If it gets too hot, it burns spontaneously, causing the engine to knock (fire unevenly). However, diesel engines work differently. At first only air goes into the combustion cylinder, and this alone is compressed. The air gets very hot, so when fuel is added, combustion begins without a spark. Because of the way they work, diesel engines can reach higher burning temperatures without knocking. This is why diesel engines are more fuel-efficient.

Modern diesel vehicles, such as this Mercedes Bluetec, produce very little pollution. This is partly because modern diesel fuels are much cleaner than in the past. In addition, the Bluetec has three different catalytic converters, which remove pollutants from the exhaust gases.

CUTTING EDGE: CLEANER DIESEL

Although diesel engines are more efficient, diesel fuel produces more pollution when it burns. However, cleaner diesel fuels, and improvements in diesel engine design, are rapidly reducing the pollution that diesel engines cause.

Sadi Carnot

As a young man, Sadi Carnot trained in chemistry and physics in Paris. However, in 1815, European armies invaded France, and Carnot joined other students in the army to defend his city. He stayed in the army for most of his life. In Paris, Carnot became interested in steam engines. At the time, the most advanced steam engines were being made in Britain, and Carnot wanted to find a way of making French engines that were more efficient. Many other scientists and engineers had tackled this problem, but Carnot took a new approach. He did not carry out scientific experiments, and he ignored most of the details of how an engine works. He was the first person to focus on the vital step in the process – the fall in temperature as the steam (the working fluid) does work. He showed that the efficiency of any engine depended on the difference between the hottest and the coldest temperatures that the working fluid reached in the engine, and not on the properties of the fluid itself.

THE SCIENCE YOU LEARN:
SAVING ENERGY AT TRAFFIC LIGHTS

When a car stops at traffic lights, the engine keeps running but does no work. Nearly one-fifth of every gallon of petrol is wasted by this idling time. An ISG system avoids this problem and saves energy. ISG stands for Integrated Starter/Generator. As the name suggests, the starter motor of the vehicle is also an electricity generator. Every time the car brakes, part of the energy used for braking goes into the starter motor. The starter motor generates electricity and feeds it into the battery. When the car is stopped completely, the engine turns off, but it turns back on automatically as soon as the driver puts their foot on the accelerator. Starting the engine up time after time uses energy, but the electricity stored during braking more than makes up for these losses.

Idling at traffic lights not only wastes fuel, but also increases carbon dioxide emissions.

CUTTING EDGE: HALF THE SIZE AND TWICE THE PUNCH

American researchers Leslie Bromberg, Daniel Cohn, and John Heywood at the Sloan Automotive Laboratory of the Massachusetts Institute of Technology (MIT), are working with engineers at the Ford Motor Company to develop a new type of engine. The new engine is far more efficient than those currently in use.

The researchers have found a way to avoid knocking. Knocking makes it impossible to compress any more air in the cylinder of a petrol engine. To solve this problem, they inject a small amount of ethanol (alcohol) into the combustion cylinder when the mixture is ready to burn. The ethanol vaporizes (becomes a gas), and this cools the mixture just enough to avoid knocking.

With the knocking problem solved, it is possible to inject more air into the cylinder and compress it further before combustion. This makes the engine more efficient. The researchers are developing small engines (about 1.2 litres) that are as powerful as engines twice this size. Yet they have a fuel consumption lower than that of a small car. If tests continue to go well, the new engines could be in cars by 2012.

MIT researchers Leslie Bromberg (left), Daniel Cohn (centre), and John Heywood have developed an experimental engine that produces twice as much power as a conventional engine of the same size.

37

Other energy sources

Improving engine efficiency is only a short-term fix for our energy problems. If vehicles continue to run on fossil fuels, we are using up fuel supplies that will run out, and releasing carbon dioxide and pollutants into the air. In the longer term, we need transport that runs on cleaner forms of energy.

Clean fuel?

Fossil fuels are made from plants and animals that died millions of years ago. When fossil fuels burn, carbon that has been locked up in the fuel for millions of years is released into the air as carbon dioxide. Burning fossil fuels increases the overall amount of carbon dioxide in the atmosphere.

In vehicles, one way to avoid this problem is to use fuels made from plants grown today. As they grow, plants take in carbon dioxide from the air and turn it into plant **tissue**. If the plants are burned as fuel, they only release the carbon dioxide they took in as they grew. If new plants are grown to replace the ones that are burned, they will take in carbon dioxide from the air. Overall, plant-based fuels would contribute far less to global warming.

Plants simply dried and burned are impractical replacements for fossil fuels. However, it is possible to make fuels similar to petrol and diesel from plants. They are called **biofuels**.

A car designer works on the design for a new biofuel car. →

Biofuels

Biofuels are not new. The first diesel engine was demonstrated in 1898 by Rudolph Diesel (1858–1913). It was designed to run on peanut oil, not on diesel fuel. It was only when cheap oil became available in the 1920s that diesel fuel took over.

In the 1970s in Brazil, another type of biofuel was made by **fermenting** sugar cane. This fuel was **ethanol**, and was used as a substitute for petrol. Today, ethanol is a widely used fuel in Brazil, and most Brazilian cars can run on either ethanol or petrol.

Biofuels are becoming more popular both in Europe and in North America. In the United States, ethanol made from corn is the most widely used biofuel, while in Europe, **biodiesel** made from plant oils is more common. However, the amount of carbon dioxide a biofuel saves depends on how the biofuel is made (see page 40). Researchers are working on new biofuels that can be made from waste materials, or from plants such as switchgrass that can grow on waste land.

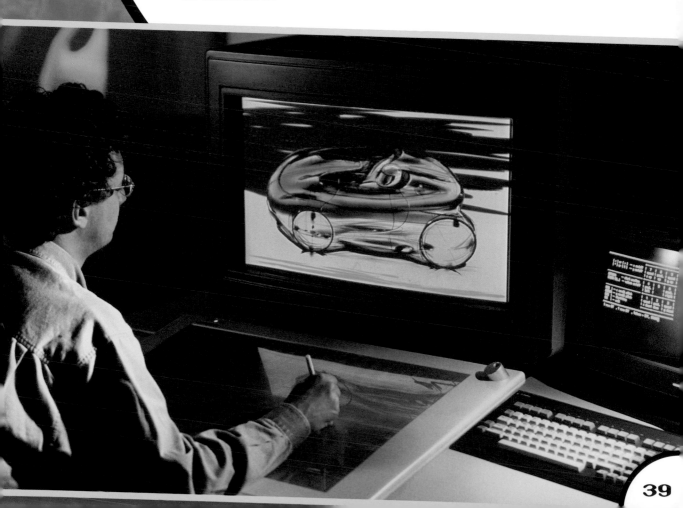

IN THE NEWS:
THE PROBLEM WITH BIOFUELS

Biofuels could be a clean, green source of energy, or a cause of misery and environmental damage on a global scale. It all depends on how they are produced.

Growing crops such as corn and sugar cane to make biofuels uses a lot of land. This land could be used to grow food. If farmers get more money to grow biofuel than to grow food, it could result in food shortages. This is unlikely to happen in developed countries where there is currently spare farmland. However, in less economically developed countries, food crops are already being uprooted to make way for biofuel crops, and this could cause serious food shortages.

A further problem is that oil-guzzling machinery and oil-based chemicals are used to grow biofuel crops. In Europe, rapeseed oil is made into biodiesel. But growing the rapeseed crop requires tractors, combine harvesters, fertilizers, and pesticides. All these factors involve the production of carbon dioxide.

Palm oil is a cheaper alternative to rapeseed oil. It is grown in tropical countries. However, rainforests are cut down to grow the palm oil crops, which causes further damage to the environment.

If biofuels are to be useful, they must be produced in ways that do not use good farmland or damage the environment. Researchers are developing ways to make biofuels from fast-growing grasses, which can grow on poor farmland and give high yields in a short time. Another area of research involves the use of algae (microscopic water plants) or other microbes to produce biofuels. In the longer term this may prove to be the best solution.

The Tesla Roadster is a new electric car based on the Lotus Elise sports car. Extra-light materials and the latest battery technology give the Tesla the performance of a sports car.

Batteries and hybrids

Electricity can be used to power cars. Even if the electricity is made using fossil fuels, a car powered by an electric motor uses less energy than a car powered by a heat engine. This is because even the best engines are only about 30 percent efficient, whereas electric motors can be more than 90 percent efficient.

Car manufacturers have produced experimental electric cars for many years. In terms of price per mile travelled, energy efficiency, and emissions electric cars perform much better than cars with IC engines, but they are seen as slow. Now, manufacturers have developed **hybrid vehicles**. These cars are driven by a combination of battery power and a small IC engine. At slow speeds, the car runs mainly on battery power. When speed or acceleration is needed, the engine adds its power to that of the batteries.

Fuel cells

Fuel cells could power vehicles of the future. Fuel cells are similar to batteries, but they use fuel like an engine, instead of needing to be recharged. The big advantage they have over heat engines is that they do not burn their fuel to produce heat. Instead, they convert the fuel to electricity. The electricity is then used to power an electric motor. As with battery power, fuel cells are more efficient than IC engines. The first successful fuel cell was built by British engineer Tom Bacon (1904–1992) in 1959.

Fuel cells can provide more power than batteries, and modern fuel-cell cars can match the performance of a conventional car. However, fuel cells are currently very expensive to make. They are unlikely to replace conventional cars until they are much cheaper.

Fuel cells usually run on hydrogen fuel. The only waste product from a fuel cell is water. However, hydrogen is expensive to make and store, and currently it is most easily made from fossil fuels. This further problem must be overcome before fuel-cell vehicles can fully replace conventional vehicles.

A bus called the ThunderPower was the first fuel-cell bus to run on a commercial bus route. The bus was tested for six months in California, USA, in 2002–3. Other buses have since been tested in several European cities and in Perth, Australia.

THE SCIENCE YOU LEARN: HOW DO FUEL CELLS WORK?

A fuel cell works by separating atoms of hydrogen into two parts, then putting them back together. Hydrogen is the simplest kind of atom. It has just two parts – a positively charged **proton** at the centre, which is circled by a negatively charged **electron**. In a fuel cell, the protons and electrons are separated by a membrane. The protons can go through the membrane, but the electrons cannot. Instead, the electrons have to go a longer way round, through a wire. Electrons moving through a wire make an electric current, so the fuel cell produces electricity. On the other side of the fuel cell, the protons and electrons join up with oxygen to form water.

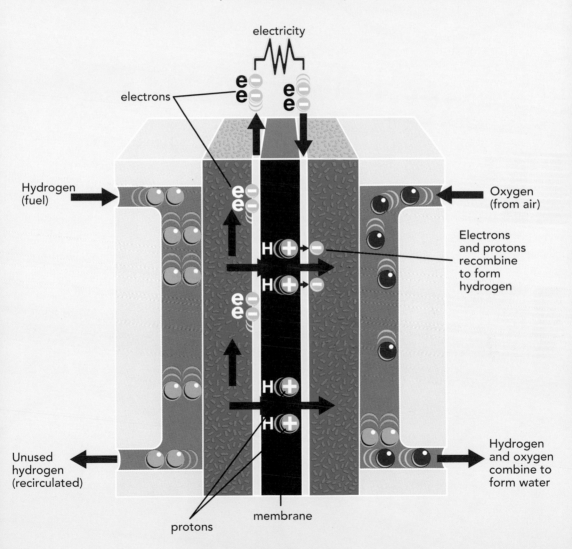

electricity

electrons

Hydrogen (fuel)

Oxygen (from air)

Electrons and protons recombine to form hydrogen

Unused hydrogen (recirculated)

Hydrogen and oxygen combine to form water

protons

membrane

The H-racer uses hydrogen fuel and is powered by a fuel cell. It has its own solar-powered refuelling station, which makes hydrogen from water. The H-racer is just a toy. But in the future we may all be driving cars like this.

IN THE NEWS: A COMPLEX EQUATION

Today we have a range of technologies for building greener cars and other forms of transport. However, using greener, cleaner technologies is not a straightforward solution. The costs of switching to new forms of energy will be enormous. Private companies will not make the change unless they can still make good profits. People must want to drive greener vehicles, and be willing to pay a little more for them. Governments must encourage the development of technology through grants and laws. Scientists also play a role in improving new forms of energy and providing information about their benefits and drawbacks. Lastly, environmental groups, such as Friends of the Earth and Greenpeace, must remind people of the urgency of the energy crisis, and point out shortcomings in government policies. All of these factors affect how and when a changeover to greener technologies will take place.

Japanese sailor, Ken'ichi Horie completes a solo crossing of the Pacific Ocean in his solar-powered boat, *Malt's Mermaid*.

Sun power

Electric boats have existed for many years. By fitting solar panels to an electric boat, it is possible to convert it to run at least partly on solar power. Electric boats are generally quite slow, but they are used in many parts of the world as ferries and for short cruise trips. In sunny places, such as Australia and the Caribbean, electric ferries and cruise ships running on solar power have been either converted or built from scratch.

Solar boats can also function in less sunny places. *SolarShuttle* is an electric cruise boat that runs entirely on solar power. It is used on a lake in Hyde Park in London. Solar boats have also made much longer voyages. In 1996, Japanese sailor Ken'ichi Horie crossed the Pacific Ocean in a solar-powered boat made from recycled aluminium cans. In 2007, a catamaran called *Sun21* carried five people across the Atlantic Ocean using entirely solar power.

CUTTING EDGE: GREEN SPACEFLIGHT?

Virgin Galactic is a private company that is developing what could be the world's first green spaceship. They hope that the spaceship, *SpaceShip 2*, will take tourists on short rides into space. *SpaceShip 2* is a larger version of *SpaceShip One*, an award-winning spaceship built by designer Burt Rutan. *SpaceShip 2* uses a fraction of the fuel needed by a conventional rocket. It manages this in two ways. Firstly, the rocket is launched from high in the atmosphere. A large conventional aircraft carries it to this height. This means that the rocket motors are needed for a much shorter time than with a ground launch. Secondly, the rocket motors are powered by a strange mixture of rubber and nitrous oxide (laughing gas), and they use less fuel than conventional rockets. However, the future of *SpaceShip 2* is currently uncertain after an explosion during engine tests killed three people.

Conclusion

We have seen how old and new ideas can be put together to design buildings that use less energy and water, and produce less waste. We have also seen that vehicles can be made lighter and more streamlined, with more efficient engines, and with less use of polluting fuels. All these ideas can help us to tackle the problems of climate change, increased pollution and waste, limited water supplies, and diminishing fossil fuels.

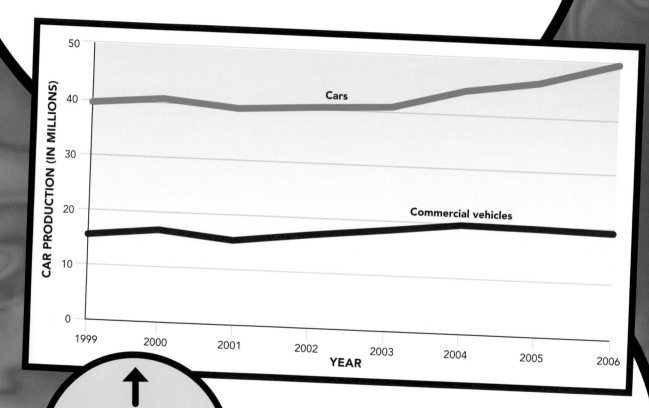

This graph shows the increase in vehicle production worldwide from 1999 to 2006.

How science helps

Science and technology can provide us with sources of clean, renewable energy to replace fossil fuels. The two main ways to tackle our energy problems are to use less energy and to find energy sources that do not harm the environment. Recycling can reduce waste, and redesigning our water systems and appliances can save water.

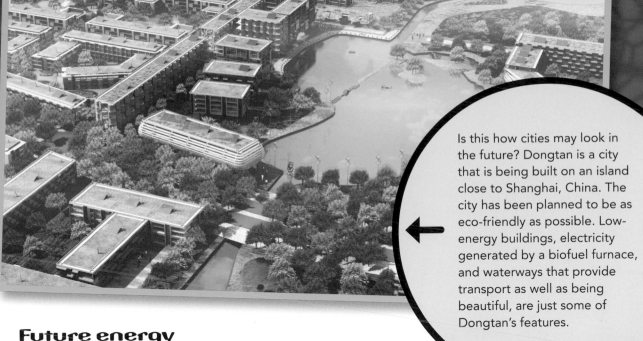

Is this how cities may look in the future? Dongtan is a city that is being built on an island close to Shanghai, China. The city has been planned to be as eco-friendly as possible. Low-energy buildings, electricity generated by a biofuel furnace, and waterways that provide transport as well as being beautiful, are just some of Dongtan's features.

Future energy

It is not likely that we will replace fossil fuels with just one source of energy. Solar and wind power for buildings, biofuels and fuel cells for transport, and other energy sources such as wave and tidal power, will all gradually increase in use as fossil fuels are phased out. Scientists may even discover new kinds of energy that we can add to the ones we already have. Scientists are already experimenting with fusion – the way that the Sun produces energy. Perhaps in the future we will be able to build tiny Suns to meet all our energy needs.

Science can be a great help in solving our energy, water, and waste problems, but it is not the complete solution. People, governments, and other organizations must all work together if we want to build a greener future.

Is this a car of the future? The MIDI-Tata air car is an experimental, low-pollution vehicle that runs on compressed air. The air is released into a cylinder similar to the combustion cylinder in an IC engine. The high-pressure air pushes down the piston without needing any combustion to make it expand.

Facts and figures

Below are some famous names in the scientific field of engineering:

Charles, Jacques Alexandre César (1746–1823)

The French chemist, physicist, and aeronaut Jacques Alexandre César Charles, was born 12 November 1746, in Beaugency, Loiret, France. Beginning as a clerk in the finance ministry, Charles turned to science and experimented with electricity. He developed several inventions, including a hydrometer, but he is best known for his formulation in 1787 of one of the basic gas laws. This is now known as Charles' law, and states that, at constant pressure, the volume occupied by a fixed weight of gas is directly proportional to the absolute temperature. However, during his lifetime, Charles was better known for inventing the hydrogen balloon.

Becquerel, Alexandre-Edmond (1820–1891)

Edmond Becquerel was one of a family of French scientists. Edmond, his father Antoine-César, and his son Henri were all physicists. By the age of 18, Edmond was working with his father at the Museum of Natural History in Paris. When his father died in 1878, Edmond took over as Director of the Museum. Edmond's main research was into electricity, magnetism, and light. In his studies on photochemistry (the effect of light on chemicals) he discovered that when light shone on some metals, an electric voltage was created across the metal. This was known as the photovoltaic effect.

Diesel, Rudolf Christian Karl (1858–1915)

Rudolph Diesel invented the diesel engine. Diesel's parents were German but he was born in France and then moved to London. At the age of 12 he was sent to live with his aunt and uncle in Germany. He began studying to be an engineer when he was 15. One of Diesel's first jobs was working for Carl von Lindé, the engineer who developed modern refrigerators. Diesel had the idea for his diesel engine in 1890, and gradually developed it over the next seven years. Its efficiency and simple design made the engine very successful, and Diesel became a rich man. Diesel's death was very mysterious. In 1913 he took a ship across the English Channel. He ate on board at around 10 p.m., then went to his cabin. When the steward went to call Diesel the next morning his cabin was empty. His body was found in the sea ten days later.

Bacon, Francis Thomas (1904-1992)

Tom Bacon was a British electrical engineer who developed the first practical fuel cells. Bacon began work on fuel cells during World War II. His idea was that they could be used to power submarines. The basic idea of the fuel cell had been demonstrated 100 years earlier, by the Welsh scientist Sir William Grove (1811–1896). However, turning Grove's discovery into a useful fuel cell proved to be a long process. Bacon tried out many combinations of materials, and solved one problem after another in his research. Eventually, after 17 years of work, he demonstrated a successful six-kilowatt fuel cell in Cambridge in 1959. Improved versions of this fuel cell were used in the Apollo space missions.

Rutan, Burt (born 1943)

Burt Rutan is an aircraft and space engineer who has designed a string of experimental and record-breaking aircraft and spacecraft. He began designing his first aircraft in his garage in 1965. He tested its streamlining by driving along with a model of the plane strapped to the top of his car. In 1974 Rutan set up his own aircraft design company. He made many successful aircraft, but his first really big success was in 1986, when his *Voyager* aircraft made the first non-stop, non-refuelled flight around the world. In 2004 Rutan's spacecraft *SpaceShip One* was the first private spacecraft to fly into space. He then began work with Virgin Galactic on *SpaceShip* 2. In 2005 another Rutan design, *GlobalFlyer*, made the first solo non-stop flight around the world.

The ten most fuel-efficient petrol vehicles

Ranking	Make	Model	Engine Capacity (cc)	CO_2 (g/km)	Fuel Consumption (mpg)
1	HONDA	Insight	995	80	83.1
2	TOYOTA	Prius	1,497	104	65.7
3	PEUGEOT	107	998	109	61.3
4	TOYOTA	Aygo	998	109	61.4
5	SMART	City Coupé Hatchback	698	113	60.1
6	DAIHATSU	Charade	989	114	58.9
7	VAUXHALL	Corsa	998	115	58.8
8	SMART	Roadster	698	116	57.6
9	HONDA	Civic IMA	1,339	116	57.6
10	DAIHATSU	Sirion	998	118	56.5

The ten most fuel-efficient diesel vehicles

Ranking	Make	Model	Engine Capacity (cc)	CO_2 (g/km)	Fuel Consumption (mpg)
1	CITROEN	C2	1,398	107	68.9
2	CITROEN	C3	1,398	109	67.3
3	RENAULT	Clio	1,461	110	67.3
4	PEUGEOT	206	1,398	113	65.6
5	RENAULT	Clio	1,461	113	65.8
6	FIAT	Panda	1,248	114	65.7
7	FORD	Fiesta	1,399	114	65.7
8	VAUXHALL	Corsa	1,248	115	65.6
9	PEUGEOT	1007	1,398	115	64.1
10	SMART	Forfour	1,493	116	64.2

Embodied energy of building materials

Dense materials have a much larger embodied energy per cubic metre, because a cubic metre of a dense material weighs much more than the same amount of a less dense material.

Material	Embodied energy	
	megajoules/kilo	megajoules/cubic metre
straw bales	0.24	31
soil-cement (rammed earth)	0.42	819
local stone	0.79	2,030
concrete blocks	0.94	2,350
timber	2.5	1,380
brick	2.5	5,170
recycled aluminium	8.1	21,870
recycled steel	8.9	37,210
plywood	10.4	5,720
glass	15.9	37,550
steel	32.0	251,200
PVC	70.0	93,620
copper	70.6	631,164
paint	93.3	117,500
aluminium	227	515,700

Find out more

Books

Causing a Stink: The Eco Warriors' Handbook, Caroline Clayton (Bloomsbury, 1996)

Garbage Disposal (Action for the Environment), Deborah Jackson Bedford
(Smart Apple Media, 2005)

Global Cities (Project Eco-City), Philip Parker (Thomson Learning, 1995)

Renewable Energy (Energy Essentials), Nigel Saunders and Steven Chapman
(Raintree, 2004)

Our Environment: Greener Cars, Karen D. Povey (Kidhaven Press, 2006)
Eco: Environmentally Friendly Design and Decoration, Elizabeth Wilhide
(Quadrille Publishing, 2004)

Websites

- http://www.oberlin.edu/ajlc/ajlcHome.html
  The Adam Joseph Lewis Center for Environmental Studies. Find out all about a
  real low-energy building. See how much energy the building uses each day, or
  what happens to the waste water.

- http://www.cat.org.uk/links/links_content.tmpl?init=1&subdir=links&dir=links
  Website of the Centre for Alternative Technology (CAT). Links to websites on
  energy efficiency, low-energy building, waste, recycling, and other topics from
  CAT.

- http://www.fueleconomy.gov/
  Drivers can find out how fuel-efficient their cars are on this website. You can also
  watch videos of the world's most fuel-efficient vehicles.

- http://www.wasteonline.org.uk/
  A website about waste and what we can do about it.

- http://www.wsc.org.au/
  World Solar Challenge: a race across Australia in solar cars, held every autumn.

- http://www.wrap.org.uk/
  The website for WRAP. Learn about low-energy materials, composting,
  packaging, and recycling projects.

Places to visit

- Centre for Alternative Technology, Machynlleth, Powys, Wales SY20 9AZ. Since it began in 1973, CAT has been an international centre for developing environmental technology. Visit their website at www.cat.org.uk/index.tmpl to learn more about paying a visit.

- Find an eco-home or Eco-village near you. Global EcoVillage Network is a network connecting places around the world where people are trying to live a low-energy, eco-friendly lifestyle. If you go to their website (http://gen.ecovillage.org/about/index.html) you can look up an eco-village near you. Many villages have tours and events you can go to.

- The Pacific Wheel, Pacific Park, Santa Monica Pier, California, USA. The world's first solar-powered Ferris wheel!

- NREL Visitors Center, 15013 Denver West Parkway, Golden, Colorado 80401-3393, USA. NREL is the National Renewable Energy Laboratory. Learn all about renewable energy at their low-energy Visitor Centre. Even the website (http://www.nrel.gov/) is powered by renewable energy.

Glossary

acid rain   type of air pollution that makes the rain in an area more acidic

aerodynamic   having a streamlined shape that moves smoothly through air

atoms   very tiny particles that everything is made of

biodiesel   type of biofuel that can be used instead of diesel oil

biofuels   fuels made from plant or animal material that can be used to power cars and other vehicles

carbon footprint   amount of carbon dioxide produced in the course of making or doing something

carbon neutral   balancing the amount of carbon dioxide released into the atmosphere from burning fossil fuels by using renewable energy

climate change   changes in the Earth's climate caused by human actions

condense   turn from a gas into a liquid

drag   the friction force that resists the movement of an object through a liquid or gas

drought   lack of rainfall

electron   part of an atom. Electrons are much smaller than protons, they have a negative charge, and they orbit round the nucleus.

ethanol   type of biofuel that can be used instead of petrol

evaporate   turn from a liquid into a gas

ferment   to grow bacteria or other microbes in conditions where there is little or no air

fossil fuel   oil, gas, or coal. These are all fuels formed from the remains of animals and plants that lived millions of years ago.

friction   the rubbing of one object or surface against another

fuel cell   power source that uses hydrogen or another fuel to produce electricity

green energy   energy (usually electricity) produced by a method such as solar or wind power, which does not use fossil fuels and does not cause pollution or environmental damage

heat capacity   capacity of a material to soak up and retain heat

hybrid vehicle   vehicle that is powered by a mixture of electric power and an IC engine

insulation   an insulating material is one that does not allow heat to pass through it easily

internal combustion (IC) engine   engine that works by exploding fuel inside a closed combustion chamber

kinetic energy   the energy of a moving object

lift   in aerodynamics, lift is a force that tends to lift an aircraft into the air

monitor   to keep a check on

ore   kind of rock that is rich in metal or minerals

photovoltaic (PV) cell   type of battery that produces electricity when light falls on it

potential energy   stored energy; for example, a rock at the top of a hill has gravitational potential energy

proton   part of an atom. Protons are found in the nucleus (centre) of the atom and have a positive charge.

radiation   light, or other similar kinds of invisible rays, such as ultraviolet and radio waves

selenium   an element (a simple chemical made from one type of atom) similar to sulphur

semiconductor   material such as silicon or germanium, used in electronic components

status symbol   something that shows a person's position in society

tissue   in biology, the living material that an animal or plant is made of

triple-glazed   windows with three panes of glass, separated from each other by thin gaps

vacuum   an empty space

Index